WITH ALL MY LOVE

By the same author:

Do You Love Me?
Late Have I Loved You
One of Those who Said Yes
Be Happy
The Golden Rule

MARIAROSA GUERRINI O.S.A.

With all my love

THE PSALMS

ST PAULS

Original title: *Ti amo, Signore, mia forza*
© Editrice Rogate, Roma, 1988

Translated by Thomas Kala

Cover by Mary Lou Winters fsp
based on design by Mariarosa Guerrini

ST PAULS
Middlegreen, Slough SL3 6BT, United Kingdom
Moyglare Road, Maynooth, Co. Kildare, Ireland

English translation © ST PAULS (UK) 1992

ISBN 085439 411 7

First published 1992. Reprinted 1995

Printed by The Guernsey Press Co., Guernsey, C.I.

ST PAULS is an activity of the priests and brothers of
the Society of St Paul who proclaim the Gospel through the
media of social communication

To Mother Alexandra
and to all those
who have helped me to love God

The *Psalms* are the hymns and prayers of the Bible. There are hymns of praise and worship of God; prayers for help, protection, and salvation; pleas for forgiveness; songs of thanksgiving. But the theme that dominates all others in the Psalms is the love of God.

Introduction

When the HAND of God fashioned
the universe and all things in it,
their beauty was truly stunning.
The sun, the moon, the stars,
the peace and silence of firmament
surrounded the earth
bursting with life:
the joy of colours,
the endless variety of species,
the sea with its inexhaustible riches.
All these
only an infinite love
could have brought into existence.

But love was alone,
there was no response,
no dialogue.

Then the HAND of God
formed the first man,
and God spoke with man
and, how stupendous,
man spoke with God.

There was born a covenant
between them,
in love and for all time:

> 'I am setting my bow in the clouds,
> it shall be the sign of the covenant
> between me and the world'
> (Gen 9:13).

Like a loving caress of the Father,
the Lord's blessing rested on man.
This paternal HAND of God
is always with us,
lighting our path,
easing our journey,
wiping away our tears,
protecting us from dangers,
sharing our joys,
offering us refuge
every moment of our life.

To discover
and enjoy God's love
is true JOY!

God is loved
not in particular places
nor through endless searching.

God is heard
not in words
nor in footsteps.

God is recognized
in the footprints
of Love
promenading in your heart.

St Augustine, *Discourse 23*

I love you,
O Lord,
my strength,
my rock,
my deliverer,
my God,
my refuge,
my shield,
my bulwark,
my salvation.

Psalm 18

My heart
overflows
with beautiful words,
as I compose
this song
for my king.

Psalm 45

You have put
more joy
in my heart
than all the
corn and wine
could ever offer.

Psalm 4

I will praise you,
Lord,
with all my heart;
I will tell
of all your wonderful deeds.
I will sing
with joy because of you.
I will praise
your name,
Almighty God.

Psalm 9

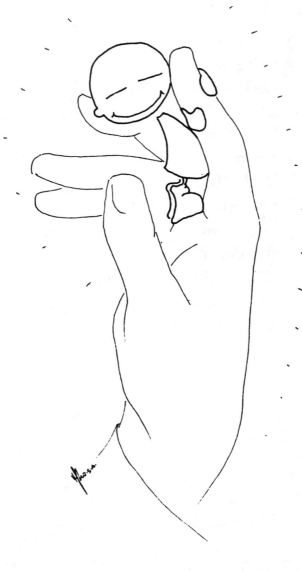

I will sing
and make melody
and praise you, O God.
Wake up,
my soul!
Wake up,
my harp and lyre!
I will wake up
the dawn.
And I will praise you,
O Lord,
among the nations.

Psalm 57

At my birth
you were my protection,
and when I was a baby
you watched over me.
And since the day
I was born
you have been
my God.

Psalm 22

In the shadow
of your wings
I sing for joy.

I cling to you,
and your hand
upholds me.

Psalm 63

You give me strength,
and make my path safe.
You make me
sure-footed as a deer,
and hold me safe
on high mountains.

Psalm 18

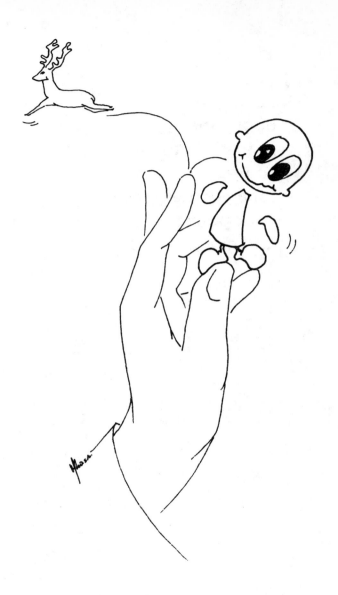

I have gazed
upon you
in the sanctuary
so that
I may contemplate
your power
and glory.

Psalm 63

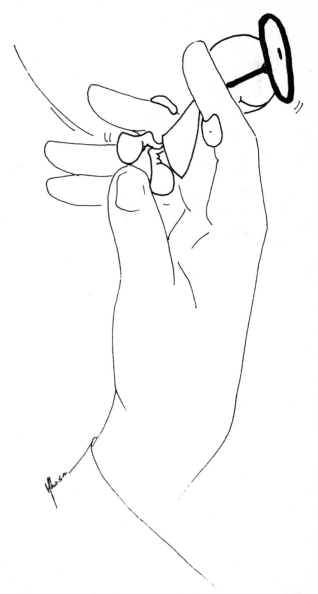

I will run
on the course
of your
commandments,
since
you have
set me free.

Psalm 119

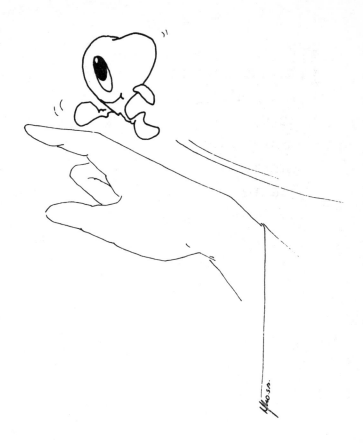

You have made
my path
safe,
and my feet
have not
faltered.

Psalm 18

If I fall
I do not
crash
to the ground,
for the Lord
sustains me.

Psalm 37

The Lord
is our guide
for ever.

Psalm 48

I love the Lord
because
he hears
my prayer.
He listens to me
whenever
I call to him.

Psalm 116

The Lord
reached down
from heaven
and took hold
of me.

Psalm 18

O Lord,
you have
delivered me
from hell
and restored me
to life.

Psalm 30

You give me
your saving shield,
your right hand
upholds me;
and your bounty
nourishes me.

Psalm 18

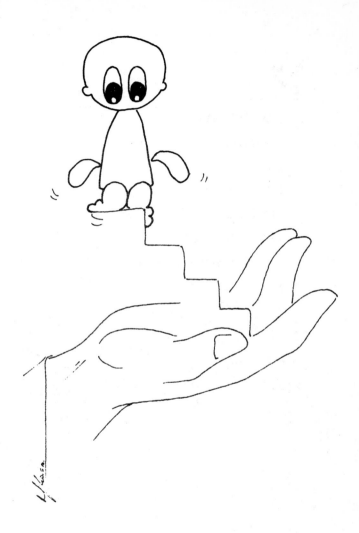

Probe
my heart,
visit me
by night,
test me
by fire –
you will find
no wickedness
in me.

Psalm 17

You are
my heritage
and my cup;
my future
is in
your hands.

Psalm 16

I waited
patiently
for the Lord;
and he
listened
to me
and heard
my cry.

Psalm 40

The Lord
is
my shield;
he saves
the upright
in heart.

Psalm 7

He hides me
in his shelter
in the day
of trouble;
he keeps me
safe
under
the cover
of his tent.

Psalm 27

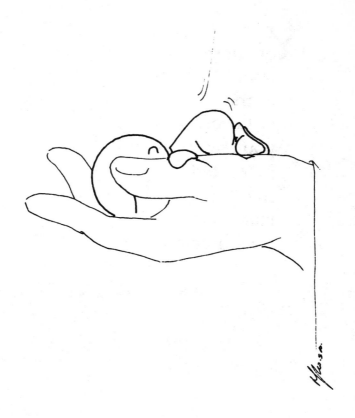

You were
good
to me,
O Lord;
you
protected
me
like
a mountain fortress.

Psalm 30

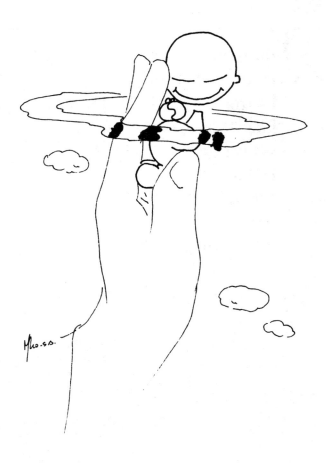

The Lord
is my shepherd;
I shall
lack
nothing
in his
pastures.

Psalm 23

As

the deer
longs for
flowing streams,
so
I long
for you,
O God.

Psalm 42

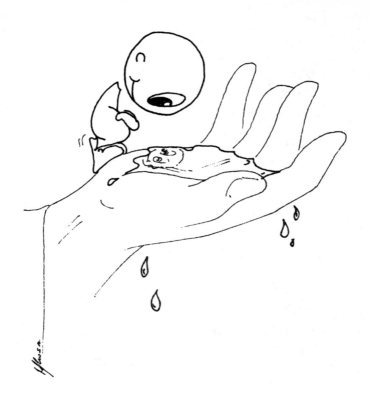

You
have
made
me
as strong as
a wild ox;
you
have
blessed
me
with happiness.

Psalm 92

I rejoice
in your
promises,
like one
who finds
a vast treasure.

Psalm 119

Like
a green
olive tree
growing
in the house
of the Lord,
I put
my trust
in his
true love.

Psalm 52

Lord,
how
I love
your
commandments;
I will
meditate
on them
all day long.

Psalm 119

You
bless
those
who obey you,
Lord;
like
a shield
your love
protects them.

Psalm 5

It is better
to trust
in the
Lord
than
to depend
on men.

Psalm 118

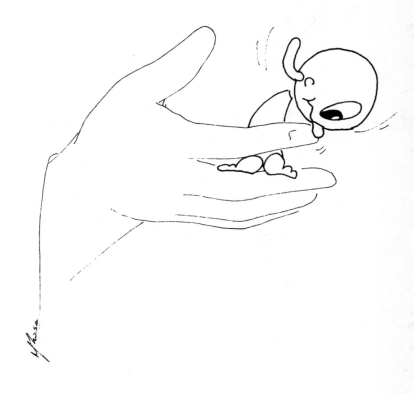

You
take
notice of
trouble
and suffering;
and
you are
always
ready
to help.

Psalm 10

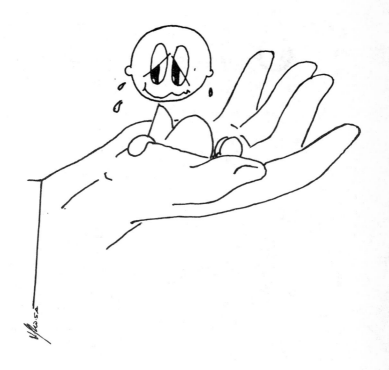

O Lord,
you
give me
light;
you
dispel
my darkness.

Psalm 18

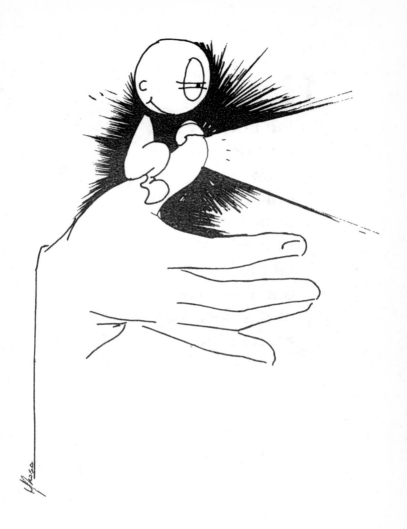

I have asked
the Lord
for one thing;
I ask
only this:
to live
in the Lord's house
all my life
and to marvel
at the goodness
of the Lord.

Psalm 27

Love
the Lord,
all his
faithful
people;
the Lord
protects
the steadfast.

Psalm 31

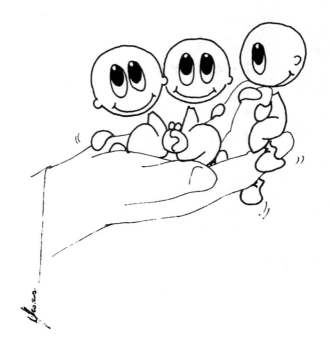

Your hands
have made
and
fashioned me.
Give me
understanding
that I may
learn
your commandments.

Psalm 119

Lord,
your love
is eternal;
do not abandon
the work
of your hands.

Psalm 138

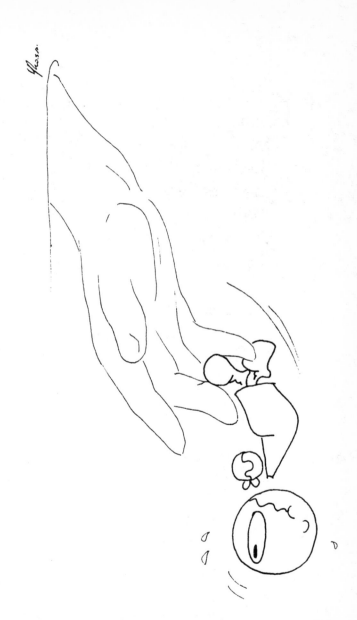

I wait
for
the Lord
more eagerly
than
watchmen
wait
for
the dawn.

Psalm 130

The Psalm
on the Love of God

I love you, O Lord,
my strength, my rock,
my deliverer, my God,
my refuge, my shield,
my bulwark, my salvation.

My heart overflows
with beautiful words,
as I compose this song
for my king.

You have put more joy
in my heart
than all the corn and wine
could ever offer.

I will praise you, Lord,
with all my heart;
I will tell
of all your wonderful deeds.

I will sing with joy
because of you.
I will praise your name,
Almighty God.

I will sing and make melody
and praise you, O God.
Wake up, my soul!
Wake up, my harp and lyre!
I will wake up the dawn.
And I will praise you, O Lord,
among the nations.

At my birth you were my protection,
and when I was a baby
you watched over me.
And since the day I was born
you have been my God.

In the shadow of your wings
I sing for joy.
I cling to you,
and your hand upholds me.

You give me strength,
and make my path safe.
You make me sure-footed as a deer,
and hold me safe on high mountains.

I have gazed upon you
in the sanctuary
so that I may contemplate
your power and glory.

I will run on the course
of your commandments,
since you have set me free.

You have made my path safe,
and my feet have not faltered.

If I fall
I do not crash to the ground
for the Lord sustains me.

The Lord
is our guide for ever.

I love the Lord
because he hears my prayers.
He listens to me whenever I call to him.

The Lord reached down from heaven
and took hold of me.

O Lord,
you have delivered me from hell
and restored me to life.

You give me your saving shield,
your right hand upholds me;
and your bounty nourishes me.

Probe my heart,
visit me by night,
test me by fire –
you will find no wickedness in me.

You are my heritage and my cup;
my future is in your hands.

I waited patiently for the Lord;
and he listened to me and heard my cry.

The Lord is my shield;
he save the upright in heart.

He hides me in his shelter
in the day of trouble;
he keeps me safe
under the cover of his tent.

You were good to me, O Lord;
you protected me
like a mountain fortress.

The Lord is my shepherd;
I shall lack nothing in his pastures.

As the deer longs for flowing streams,
so I long for you, O God.

You have made me
as strong as a wild ox;
you have blessed me with happiness.

I rejoice in your promises,
like one who finds a vast treasure.

Like a green olive tree
growing in the house of the Lord,
I put my trust in his true love.

Lord,
how I love your commandments,
I will meditate on them all day long.

You bless those who obey you, Lord;
like a shield your love protects them.

It is better to trust in the Lord
than to depend on men.

You take notice of trouble and suffering;
and you are always ready to help.

O Lord,
you give me light;
you dispel my darkness.

I have asked the Lord for one thing;
I ask only this:
to live in the Lord's house all my life
and to marvel
at the goodness of the Lord.

Love the Lord,
all his faithful people;
the Lord protects the steadfast.

Your hands
have made and fashioned me.
Give me understanding
that I may learn your commandments.

Lord,
your love is eternal;
do not abandon the work of your hands.

I wait for the Lord more eagerly
than watchmen wait for the dawn.

Be happy

The key to happiness is to be found in our own hearts. This is the message of this happy, humorous, little book. The theme of happiness is developed from the Beatitudes and various other quotations from the Bible. These beautiful thoughts and cartoons lead us to the final conviction that there can be no happiness without love and that therefore happy are those who love God and their fellow human beings.

Late have I loved you

We all need someone to whom we can relate with our human experience, who shows us the way to find our true selves, who goes before us in the stupendous and arduous ways of God.

St Augustine has always been, for many, this Someone. His message, presented here in delightful images, is drawn mainly from the *Confessions of St Augustine,* one of the few books that still succeed in touching the heart of contemporary man and woman.

Do you love me?

The call of the Gospel and Peter's response of love illustrated with an admirable sense of humour…

The fascinating adventure of following Jesus and the sweeping message of his teaching are, here, narrated by Peter, the apostle who experienced the unutterable joy of the answer to the call of the Lord.

Peter's is the story of impassioned love – unique. Reading its pages, everyone will be able to grasp the criterion and the measure of true and real love.

One of those who said YES

This is the **story of a call**, the 'inner' story of a **YES**, in which, we are sure, all those 'who have been called' will see themselves identified, and to which others will certainly respond with shared feelings.

The Golden Rule

To be truly happy we don't need to have more: we've already got too many unnecessary things. What we need is to 'live' more, to be more fully ourselves. This *Golden Rule* does not propose austere extravaganzas, but eight simple recipes for wisdom.